# Papa's House in The Country

Written by:

Suzanne Badertscher

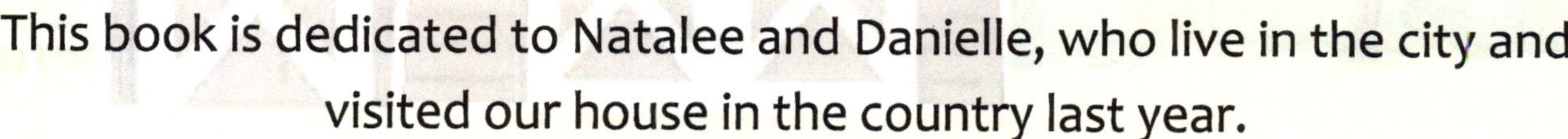

This book is dedicated to Natalee and Danielle, who live in the city and visited our house in the country last year.

# About the Author

The author is a Mom, Grandma and Great-grandma (Mema). She has written three children's books, all inspired by and written for her children. They were written to encourage kindness, respectfulness and courage. The author's children are now grown and have children of their own. It is the author's hope that other children will enjoy her stories as much as her own children and grandchildren have over the years.

This is a story about a little boy, Justin, who is eight years old, and his sister, Melissa, who is six years old. Justin and Melissa live on the ninth floor of a very nice apartment building in New York City. They are very used to city things like elevators, department stores, sidewalks, streetlights, and taxicabs.

Sometimes, Justin and Melissa go to the park in the city with their mother or father, or sometimes with their nanny, which is a city word for a babysitter. The park is one of the places where Justin and Melissa go to play in the city. It has green grass and trees, swings and seesaws, and wide sidewalks for roller-blading, skateboarding, and bike riding. The park even has a small pond for sailing toy boats in the summer and ice-skating in the winter.

After playing in the park, Justin and Melissa go back to their apartment on the ninth floor, where they play with their video and computer games or watch TV. Justin and Melissa are very happy in the city and never think about what it could be like to live in the country. In fact, they have never actually seen the country except on TV. All of that is going to change because they will soon have an adventure. They are going to take a trip to see their grandfather at his house in the country.

"But, Mommy," Justin protested, "we don't want to leave the city now. It's almost Christmas, and we'll miss everything! We always go to see the big tree in Times Square on Christmas Eve, and Santa won't be able to find us in the country! Santa knows we live here. He always comes here!"

"Now, Justin." Said his mother calmly, "Think about Santa Claus for a moment. He knows where the children are, whether they are in the country or the city. Do you believe that Santa Claus is magic?"  Justin began to think about what his mother was saying. "Do you believe that he has magic dust to sprinkle on the reindeer so they can fly and that he has a magic bag of toys that stays full to the top no matter how many toys he takes out to give to the children?"Justin was very interested now in what his mother was saying because he and Melissa had sent their letters to Santa and were very specific about what they would like to find under the tree on Christmas morning. She went on, "Do you believe that he can fly all around the world and visit every house where there are children who believe in him in just one night?"

Justin's eyes were wide with wonder as he thought about flying around the world with Santa in his sleigh and said, "Yes, I believe that, and so does Melissa ."

As she gently pushed him back onto his pillow and tucked him in, his mother went on, "And, do you believe that he sees you when you're sleeping, and he knows when you're awake? He knows if you've been good or bad, so it's time to go to sleep. We have a very big day tomorrow. We have to take a taxi to the airport, and then get on a plane. Then we'll take another taxi to the station and get on a train, and finally, we will meet your grandfather and go to his house in the country."

Justin settled down under the covers and listened quietly to his mother's voice. "You know Papa can't wait to see you and Melissa. You were very small when he was here to visit us in the city, and he has been very lonely since grandmother went to heaven last year. He is really looking forward to our visit."

Justin sighed and tried once again to talk his mother out of going to the country for Christmas. "But, we don't even know Papa, except for talking on the phone on our birthday. He seems very old in the pictures you took last year. He probably doesn't want to have kids around, making a lot of noise and everything."

Just then, Father came into the room. "Settle down, young man. Your sister is already sleeping, and as your mother said, we have a big day tomorrow." Justin's father leaned over to tousle his son's hair. "Besides, you're going to like the country. When your Aunt Jane and I were young, we had great fun there. Why, I can't remember a single Christmas when Santa didn't find our house. You'll see. Think of this trip as an adventure."

So Justin said goodnight and closed his eyes. He tried to think about Christmas at Papa's house in the country, but all he could think of was the Video Command Center that he had asked Santa for in his letter. Even if Santa found Papa's house in the country, what could he do with the command center and no video game?

The next morning, he awoke very early and ran to Melissa's room to wake her, too. "Melissa, wake up!"

"I don't want to wake up. I was dreaming about the Little Tots CD Computer Game that Santa would bring to me. I can't wait to play!" Melissa rubbed her eyes and sat up.

Justin jumped onto the foot of her bed and whispered, "It won't matter if he does bring it 'cause Papa doesn't have a computer!"

"Oh, you're right." she cried, "I won't be able to play for two whole weeks! Whatever will we do at Papa's house in the country for two weeks? He doesn't even have cable!"

Justin and Melissa decided that they had to tell Santa where they were going, so Justin wrote a note and left it by the Christmas tree in their apartment on the ninth floor of the city. The note said, "Gone to Papa's house in the country for Christmas."

Justin and Melissa worried all the way to the country. They worried in the taxi, on the plane and on the train. Finally, they arrived at the station where Papa was going to meet them. From across the train station, they heard a booming voice. "Hello! There you are!"

Justin and Melissa turned to see a big man with a beard coming toward them. Their father rushed to meet him and hugged him. So did their mother. They looked at each other as if to say, this must be Papa.

Soon, he was next to them, bending over so that he could get very close. Then he said, "This can't be Justin and Melissa! Why, Justin is just a little boy, and Melissa is only a baby! This boy is too tall and strong to be little Justin, and this little girl must be a runaway princess! That's how pretty she is."

Justin and Melissa smiled. Melissa even giggled a little. Justin shook his hand and said, "How do you do, Papa?" and Melissa said, "Hi, Papa." He straightened to his full height and let out a great laugh. With that, he swooped Melissa up into the air and patted Justin on the shoulder. "Well then, let's all go home for Christmas!"

After settling into the car, Papa explained that they had to drive for about an hour to get to his house in the country. He said that everyone should just relax and enjoy the ride. Before long, Justin and Melissa fell asleep.

Gone To Papa's house in the Country for Christmas

Just for a moment, when he awoke the next morning, he thought he must still be asleep and dreaming. Airplanes suspended from the ceiling surrounded him. There was a train on winding tracks set up with miniature buildings and trees and people and a tunnel that went right under his bed. There was a wonderful building all made out of metal in one corner of the room and a large wooden horse in another corner. It had a saddle and even guns in a holster and a cowboy hat hanging on the saddle.

Justin rubbed his eyes. "Wow!" he whispered. He jumped out of the bed to get a closer look at all the wondrous things in the room. The more he looked, the more he found. At the foot of the bed was a toy box filled to the top with one interesting toy after another. "I must be dreaming!" he said aloud.

Just then, his father came into the room. "Dad, look at all this stuff!"

Justin's father laughed. "I told you it would be an adventure, and it's only just begun." "Where did all this come from?" Justin asked, still looking from one thing to another. "These things were mine when I was a boy. Your grandfather saved everything, and when he knew we were coming to visit, he brought all of this down from the attic for you."

All Justin could say was, "Wow!"

"Let's go see Melissa's room. She is staying in Aunt Jane's old room." Said father.

So they went down the hall where they found Melissa and her mother sitting at a table pretending to have tea. This room was also full of wondrous things, except they were all girl things. There were dolls and furniture to play house, a little stage with curtains and everything for a puppet show, a carousel horse, a doll house with people, and even a fake lawn and swing set for the fake kids to play on. Melissa was wearing a big hat and feathers over her pajamas and plastic high heels that looked like glass slippers. "Justin, look at all this. I think Santa already found us!"

Justin's and Melissa's mother and father smiled. Mother said, "Do you still think you will be bored at Papa's house in the country?"

"Oh no!" they both said. Melissa began to talk to the dolls now sitting at the table with her, and Justin went back to his father's old room to play with the boys' toys. Mother and Father went downstairs to have breakfast with Papa.

As the days before Christmas passed, Justin and Melissa found ever so many things to do in the country. They didn't even miss the computer and the video games or even cable TV. They went skating on the pond and slid down the hills on wooden sleds. They all went together to cut a fresh Christmas tree and drag it home behind old Nellie, the horse. Melissa and Justin got to ride on Nellie's back while everyone else walked on the top of the snow with big snowshoes. One night under a full moon, they rode in a one-horse open sleigh behind Nellie and sang Jingle Bells all the way. Another time, they made candy out of snow and maple syrup. It was good, too. They had snowball fights and made snowmen and forts. There was always something to do at Papa's house in the country.

On Christmas Eve, they all piled into the car and drove to the nearby village, where they listened to the children of the town singing Christmas songs. They shopped and had dinner at a small restaurant that Papa called 'his diner.' Father explained that Papa and Grandma had owned the diner for years, and he and Aunt Jane used to be there every day after school. They would play the jukebox and ... well that's another story...

All too soon, Christmas Day arrived. Even though they were happy that it was Christmas morning at last, as all good little children are, Justin and Melissa knew that they would be going back to the city a few days after Christmas. They were really going to miss Papa and his house in the country. They had nearly forgotten about the Video Command Center and the Little Tots CD Computer Game that they had asked Santa for in their letters.

Nevertheless, as they neared the bottom stair, they became excited and raced into the living room where the freshly-cut, decorated, and brightly lighted tree stood. Beneath the tree was a Video Command Center complete with controls and a helmet. Next to it, there was a Little Tots CD Computer Game with all the interactive doll accessories that Melissa had dreamed of.

When Papa, Mother, and Father came into the room, Justin and Melissa were looking first at their new toys and then at each other and back again. Mother said, "Well, you two, what do you think now? Santa found you with no trouble at all."

"He sure did and gave us just what we asked for." Melissa looked at Justin to see what he would say. He said, "Let's see what you got for Christmas!" They began to bring wrapped presents to the grown-ups and made little piles of wrapped presents on the floor for themselves. At the back of the tree, Justin found two very large boxes. They were too heavy for Melissa. Even when Justin helped, they were hard to move.

COM
CENTRE
LITTLE TOT

Papa offered to·help and dragged them into the middle of the room. "Well, let's see who these are for?" Papa said, with a wink at Father and Mother. "Justin and Melissa were almost jumping up and down as Papa read the tags. They both said, "To Justin and Melissa, from Santa Claus."

"Oh, let's see, let's see!" they shouted. Together, they ripped off the paper. They soon discovered that Santa had brought them a Satellite Dish and a Computer! Everyone laughed because they all knew that the gifts were really for Papa.

Justin and Melissa spent the rest of the morning teaching Papa how to surf the channels, play video games, and use the computer. They had a lot of fun but soon tired of it. Justin and Melissa begged to go outside. They didn't want to waste one-minute doing city things while they were in the country. During the rest of the visit, they played with the toys from Papa's attic and played outside whenever they could. Each day, they would spend a little time showing Papa how to use the computer so he could send e-mail and pictures to them in the city.

When it was time to go home, they made Papa promise that he would come to the city to visit them. He agreed, as long as they promised to come back to visit him in the country during the summer. They hugged him and squealed with joy. They couldn't wait to tell their friends in the city all about Papa's house in the country!